MW01639954

Takako and the Great Typhoon

Written by Kelly Garcia
Illustrated by Carmen Daniel

For my baby boy, Gabriel Mateo
-K.G.

This project was far from a solitary effort. Heaps of thanks to everyone who pushed, questioned, critiqued, encouraged and supported us throughout. Carmen wishes to thank her family and friends, who have supported her throughout the years. Erin thanks her husband and family for their unconditional support. Kelly thanks Kay for helping her find "the answer" to the story, her parents for teaching her everywhere can be home, and especially her husband, Joe, for being there every step of the way.

Hai-Sai Publishing
Fletcher, North Carolina
Orders: www.shisastory.com

Printed in the United States of America

ISBN: 978-0-578-00843-1

Book design by Erin Blunt

The type was set in artcraft.
The illustrations for this book were done in charcoal and pastel.

Author's Note

Shisas are beloved figures in Okinawa, gracing rooftops, walls, entranceways and gardens throughout the islands. The statues, which resemble a cross between a lion and a dog, are protectors warding off evil. Often shisas are found in pairs near entrances to buildings or on either side of a gate; one with its mouth open to scare off bad spirits, the other with its mouth closed to keep in the good.

While the shisa's origins can be traced back hundreds of years to the guardian dogs of China, today the shisa is one of Okinawa's most recognizable symbols, spotted in the smallest alleyways to the busiest thoroughfares. Many are shaped by hand out of red clay, some are cast from ceramic molds, and still others are fashioned from leftover roof tiles. Most have a stern or angry look about them, while some shisas appear happy, even playful.

The story told in this book is not a traditional Okinawan folktale. It is a personal story—one of place and home. It's the story that opened its pages to me as I walked the narrow alleys of my neighborhood with my infant son. The passing scenes of daily life, wonderful in their mix of foreignness and familiarity, evoked feelings of wonder and excitement, community and home. I tried to etch each scene in my heart for my little boy, capturing these moments in my memory so that one day he could have a sense of his birthplace. From these walks, this book was born. I hope it brings a little of Okinawa's joy and magic to your home.

Takako lived high atop a red tile roof with her brother, Nobu. Every morning, she would wake up, stretch out her legs and gaze down upon the sleepy world waking before her.

First the blue birds twittered awake. Then the children walked slowly by on their way to school. Little cars began filling the streets. And the obaasans and ojiisans met for a morning game of gateball. Little by little the day unfolded and little Takako, from her rooftop watched it all in wonder.

One day, when the last of the schoolchildren strolled past, Takako glanced at her brother, Nobu, and sighed.

"Oh, Nobu," she said. "How I wish I could get off of this roof! There is so much happening all around the village. Look at all the people around us, going to interesting places and doing interesting things! But here we sit on the roof, day after day."

Nobu responded to his sister with his nose in the air,
"We are shisas, not little girls and boys," he said. "We can't run around the streets or play in the village. Our job is to stand by this house together to keep it safe in case something bad happens. That's been the Shisa Rule forever."

Shisas must be watchful.
Shisas must stand guard.
We must work together.
To keep the house from harm.

"Ughhh," Takako huffed.

She was so tired of her brother telling her what to do all the time. Sometimes she wanted to go down into the village just to get away from Mr. Smarty Shisa Pants. But she was scared of breaking the Oldest Shisa Rule, so she didn't go. Instead, she walked to the other side of the rooftop where she sat down and pouted for a couple of minutes until she forgot why she was mad.

Days passed and nights passed. And every day little Takako watched the people and animals living their lives in the village below. Then one morning, very early, Takako woke up before her brother. The sun was just peeping over the horizon and a fresh ocean breeze drifted past. A colorful butterfly danced by her nose and flitted to a nearby bush. Takako couldn't resist. She leapt down from the roof and chased after it.

"Yippeee!"

Takako followed the pretty butterfly through the village until it disappeared behind a garden wall.

She felt so happy and free!

"Nobu's probably still sleeping," she said to herself. "I'll just play for a few more minutes. He won't even know I'm gone."

And ignoring the stares of the other shisas in the village, she set off down the road to play just a little while more.

Takako played with the children

on their way to school.

She chased the farmers' pickup trucks

as they rumbled into the fields.

She climbed the banyan trees.

Played gateball with the old people.

And danced with the taiko drummers
practicing their Eisa songs.

Takako did everything she had been dreaming of doing for so long. And as hour after hour passed, she didn't once think about her brother, Nobu, sitting alone on the rooftop.

In fact, Takako was so busy having fun, she didn't even notice the big changes taking place all around her. The soft breezes of the morning were growing stronger and stronger. The sky was getting darker and darker. And the streets getting emptier and emptier as villagers disappeared into their houses. A great typhoon was quickly approaching the island and little Takako, far, far from home, was out in the street...alone.

Suddenly, a drop of rain fell from the sky and landed on Takako's nose. First one. Then two. Then another and another. Then all at once, the whole sky opened up and it poured down rain. Takako was frightened. "Oh no! Nobu!" Takako yelled, finally remembering her brother.

"I'm coming home! *I'm coming home!*"

Takako raced toward home as fast as she could, fighting the wind. She ran past the school house. She ran by the banyan trees. She ran by the gateball yard and the sugarcane fields and the town hall where they practiced Eisa. As she ran, the Shisa Rule repeated over and over in her head.

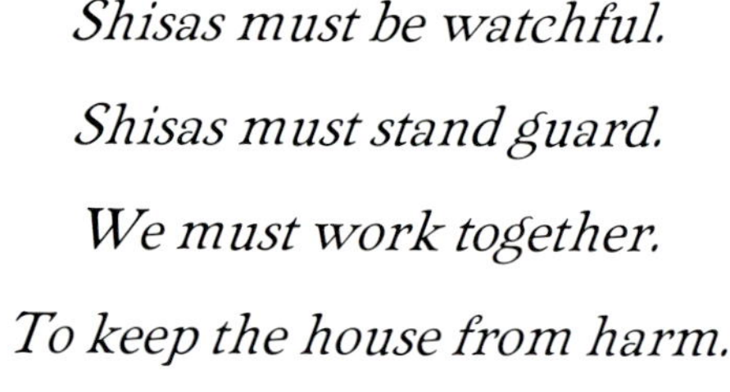

Shisas must be watchful.

Shisas must stand guard.

We must work together.

To keep the house from harm.

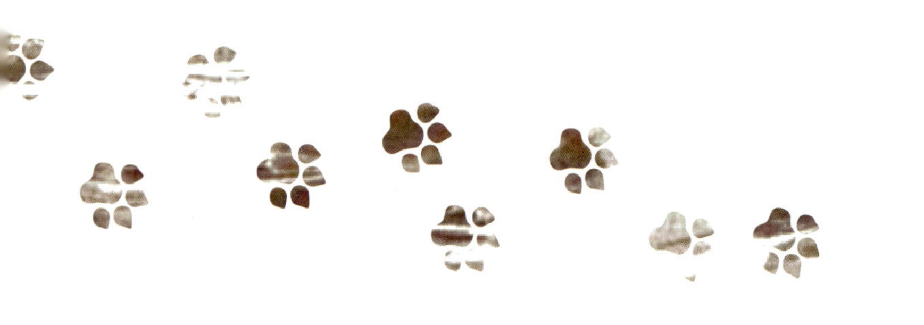

Takako ran through the alleys and down the roads and up streets until she reached her house's narrow lane. "Nobu! **Nobu!**" she shouted.

The last few feet to her house were the hardest. The wind howled and cried so loudly that Takako couldn't even hear herself yelling out for her brother. The wind gusted so hard, she had to grab onto the gates and street lamps to pull herself forward. She was so tired, she didn't know if she could make it one more step.

But just when Takako thought all her energy was gone, she looked up. There in front of her she saw her little wooden house swaying and groaning with the force of the wind. And there, holding up the whole thing, was Nobu.

"Creeeaaakkkk....grrroooaaan...." went the house.
"Creeeaaakkk....grrroooaaan....creeeaaakkk....grrroooaaan."

With each blast of wind the house leaned lower and lower on Nobu's back. Nobu shook from the effort of keeping it up. Just one more gust of wind and the house would fall!

"Nobuuuuuu!!!!" Takako yelled. Takako felt a great burst of energy and leapt forward to help her brother. As she leapt, a loud, "RRRROOOOOOAAARRRR" escaped from deep inside her body. She jumped next to Nobu and helped him push up the walls of the house.

All of a sudden, WOOOOSSSSSSHHHHHHH!!!! A powerful wind hit the two shisas and the little house.

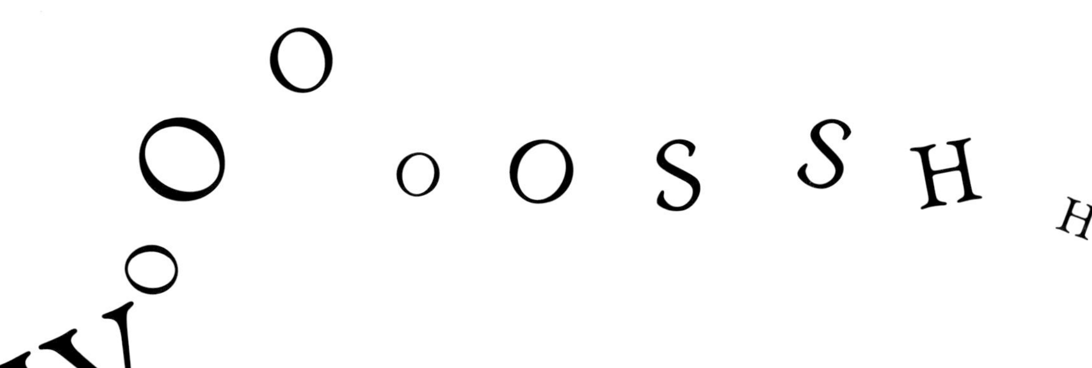

Takako and Nobu stood side by side. Using all of their strength they pushed against the walls of the little house. Little by little, the wind changed from

WOOOSSSHHH to wooossshhh

to finally to just a small *woosh,* until it died down to almost nothing at all. The rain slowed to a soft pitter patter as the great typhoon crept away from the island and slid back out to the ocean. The little house was safe.

The two shisas ran together and held each other tight. Takako felt so bad she had left Nobu by himself all day and she began to cry. Takako was sure Nobu would be angry. She had run off and broken the Shisa Rule! Nervously, she waited for Nobu to scold her. But when she looked up at him, she was amazed at what she saw. Instead of anger in Nobu's eyes, there were tears.

"Takako, thank goodness you are okay!" he said. Then he asked her a very surprising question. "How was your day?"

Takako thought about her time playing with the kids and all the people of the village, of the butterflies and trees, and then the great and scary typhoon.

"It was a BIG day," she said. "It was a GREAT, BIG day." And she realized that the very best part was being with her brother again and saving the little house with him.

Takako and Nobu climbed slowly back to the rooftop. One by one, people crept out of their homes and began cleaning up from the storm.

An orange and pink glow filled the sky and the two shisas watched as the sun set upon the village. Takako smiled. She was happy to be home.

Kelly Garcia (Author) has lived in Namihira, Yomitan since the winter of 2005. During the past three years she has taught English as a Foreign Language, worked as a picture framer, eaten her way around the island as food editor of the website Okinawa Hai, and given birth to a ten-pound son, Gabriel. Kelly admits to developing an obsession for "shisa spotting" since writing this book and is thankful that she has not yet had a car accident while on the lookout for interesting specimens! Her favorites? Two sitting on scaffolding near her house, eyes locked in a stare-down. www.shisastory.com

Carmen Daniel (Illustrator) is a registered nurse who moved to Noborikawa, Okinawa City with her husband in the spring of 2008. Art has always been a passion for Carmen although (shockingly!) she has no formal training. Fortunately, Carmen will be pursuing her passion with a new art business launching in 2009. Although Carmen has probably seen and drawn enough shisas to last a lifetime with this book, she still admits to having a few favorites: the giant red shisa at Zanpa Misaki and a cuddly mommy-baby pair in the Tsuboya Pottery District. www.carmen-daniel.com

Erin Blunt (Book Designer) is a multi-talented illustrator and graphic designer who arrived in Okinawa in the fall of 2008. She and her husband live in beautiful Nakadomari, Onna and have a gorgeous view of the East China Sea. Erin holds a BA in Illustration from the Savannah College of Art and Design and in 2007 illustrated the children's book, "Madame President". During her time in Okinawa, she plans to continue her work as a freelance artist and designer and further explore island life and culture. www.erinbluntillustration.com